The Adventures of Tovah the Therapy Dog

Tovah Visits the Library

By
Nancy Scudder

Illustrated by Casey Jo White

WINTERS PUBLISHING

winterspublishing.com

The Adventures of Tovah the Therapy Dog: Tovah Visits the Library

Text © 2023 Nancy Scudder
Illustrations © 2023 Casey Jo White

Page design by Tracy Winters

Published by:
Winters Publishing
P.O. Box 501
Greensburg, IN 47240
812-663-4948
www.winterspublishing.com

ISBN: 978-1-954116-13-9

Library of Congress Control Number: 2023932731

Printed in the United States of America

Dedicated To:

My children, Jarod, Noah, and Tristen, to whom I've read so many books when they were younger. They inspired several of the topics on each page of this book.

My name is Tovah Rae, but the children
at the library like to call me Rae Rae.
I am a certified therapy dog and my job is to provide
support, comfort, and companionship to those in need. You
may not feel well, or may be going through a
stressful time, or maybe you just need a friend to
listen and help you feel a little more confident.
I always make people smile.
I love my job.

One of my favorite things to do is visit the library. The children come in and pick out a book they would like to read. They get to practice their reading skills by reading their books to me.

Gavin likes to read books about bugs.
He tells me all of the neat things about spiders,
but the butterflies are my favorite.
Do you like bugs?
What is your favorite bug?

Caroline enjoys reading books about cats.
I like cats, but sometimes I like to bark at them.
In the library, we have to use our quiet voices.
No barking allowed!
Did you know there are therapy cats
just like us therapy dogs?

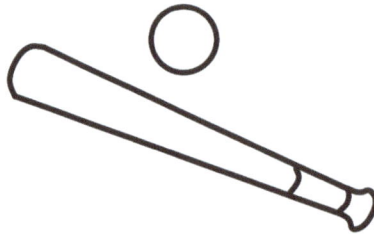

Colton's mom brings him and little Xavier to the library too. Colton hasn't learned to read yet, but he really loves books.
He brings me his favorite dinosaur books, and we look at all of the pictures and make up our own stories about them.
Dinosaurs are so cool!
Do you like dinosaurs?

Jarod always chooses books about policemen. He tells me how they help people and keep our neighborhoods safe. Jarod wants to be a policeman when he grows up.
Did you know there are specially-trained dogs that help policemen do their jobs?
I wonder if I could be a police dog.

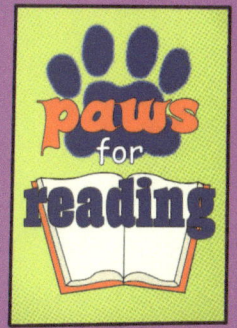

Noah and Easton like to read books about trucks.
There are so many different kinds of trucks!
We read about dump trucks, garbage trucks,
tow trucks, and semi trucks.
Monster trucks are my favorite.
What kind of trucks do you like?

Danielle and Jennifer love to read me magical
stories about a princess in a castle and unicorns.
Their books always have pretty
and colorful pictures.
I like to pretend I'm a princess in a castle.
I like unicorns, too, do you?

Tristen read a neat book to me today
about working on a farm.
I learned so many things about farming.
There are big tractors, combines, and trucks.
There is a lot of planting to be done on the farm,
so we can have fresh fruits and vegetables to eat.
Do you eat all of your vegetables at dinner time?
Green beans, corn, and broccoli
are some of my favorites!

Hailey came to the library to visit me today
and read a book about dogs.
There are so many different kinds of dogs!
There were even some just like me!
Oh, boy!
This is one of my favorite books!
Do you have a favorite book?

It's time to go home, but I had so much fun with
all of the children who shared their books with me.
The library is a great place to visit
and is full of so many wonderful stories.
Have you visited your local library?

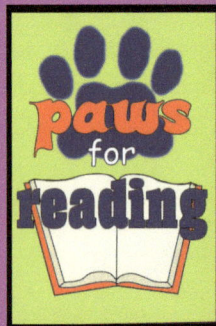

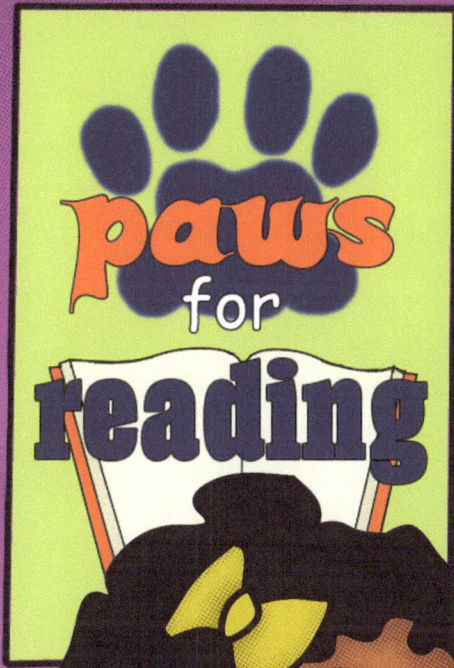

Special Thanks To:

Sue Halling and Jennifer Ison for blessing me with my best friends, Oakley and Tovah. I am so grateful for you both, for the dedication you have to the Labrador breed and rescue.

The Love On A Leash Therapy dog organization for our certification allowing us to volunteer for such a rewarding program.

Julie Pike and her beloved therapy dog, Ava. Julie formed our local chapter of Love On A Leash, Shelby County. Ava, along with Oakley and Tovah, were the founding members for Shelby County and were the beginning of our therapy dog visits to so many places. I will be forever grateful for the opportunity Julie provided all of us.

The Shelby County Public Library for allowing us to be a part of the Paws to Read program with all of the amazing children that came to visit and practice their reading skills to the dogs.

Major Health Partners for allowing Love On A Leash to be a part of the beginning of their therapy dog program and letting us bring comfort and smiles to so many patients and staff.

And, of course, to my family of canines, who on a daily basis provide adventure, comedy, comfort, dedication, love, and protection to all of us. My dog Tovah, my granddogs Kirby, Tucker, Jack, Tripp, Dottie, Zoey, K9 officer Bronco, retired K9 officer Czar, and special doggy friend, Theo.

In Loving Memory
of
Oakley

Chocolate Labrador Retriever
First therapy dog for me
Canine blood donor and superhero
4-H competitor and champion
Mentor to numerous foster dogs
Loved and missed by so many
Big brother to Tovah
My best friend

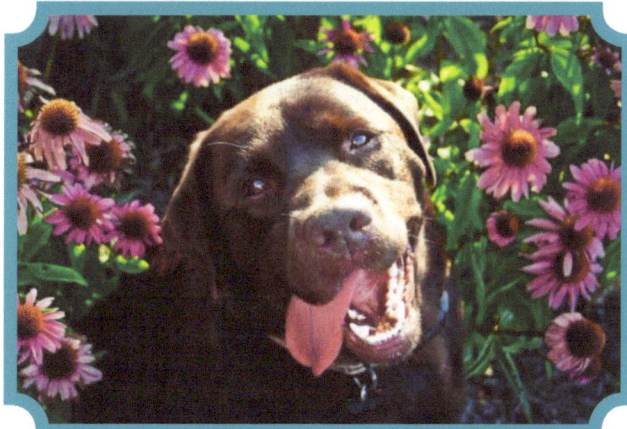

About the Author

Nancy enjoys many activities with her dog Tovah, which, along with their volunteer therapy work at the library and hospital, include many outdoor activities, trips to the beach, and of course, relaxing at home. She works full time in the medical field, is a mom to three sons, and in her free time, she loves spending time with her family. She also enjoys photography, exercise, and everything nature. Since 2010, she has continued to foster dogs for American Black and Tan Coonhound Rescue. She loves animals of every kind but most of her time has involved canines. She was a puppy raiser to service dog Holt for Canine Companions for Independence, shelter volunteer, and therapy dog handler for over 8 years. Nancy's love for Tovah is immeasurable, and she has been inspired to share some of Tovah's stories with everyone. She hopes you will enjoy their first book of adventures.

About the Illustrator

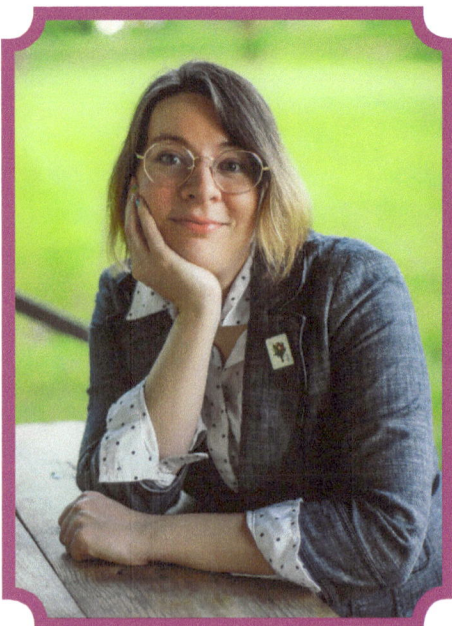

Casey Jo White is a writer who studies stamps and postal history. She enjoys learning new and interesting things and sharing them with others through writing, performing, and creating art. Her art is inspired by her favorite things: friendship, nature, fashion, travel, comics, animation, and postage stamps. She is a member of the Shelby Art Guild Association where she volunteers and displays her work. As a member of the American First Day Cover Society, she creates art for cards and envelopes that may someday go down in philatelic history.